THE ULTIMATE
Homemaking
Handbook

by

DeLayne Winmill

Illustrated by Val Chadwick Bagley

CONTENTS

Homemaking Skills

KITCHEN BASICS

Kitchen basics covers all the basic items necessary to set up housekeeping in the kitchen. You will find the necessities, specialties, and luxuries; and you can select what you have, what you need, and what you want from these lists.

MINI-CLASS IDEAS: Use the Kitchen Necessities sheet as a handout. Display several items listed. Approach the mini-class with a "Simplify your life with the basics" theme. Point out some of the advantages of a properly equipped kitchen and elaborate on some of the luxury and specialty items. This is a great "no-cost" mini-class.

KITCHEN NECESSITIES & OTHER STUFF

Kitchen Necessities

__ Knife with 12" blade for chopping
__ Knife sharpener
__ Utility or paring knife
__ Dutch oven with lid
__ 2 mixing bowls
__ Cutting board
__ 2 slotted spoons
__ 2 wooden spoons
__ 2 bowl scrapers
__ Spatula or pancake turner
__ Swivel vegetable peeler
__ Tongs
__ Measuring spoons set
__ Measuring cup set
__ Bread knife or serrated blade
__ Grater
__ Bottle opener
__ Can opener
__ Timer or clock
__ Potato masher
__ Funnel
__ Heavy-bottomed 12" frying pan
__ "No-stick" 8" frying pan
__ Extra-large soup pot
__ 2 sauce pans, small & medium
__ Colander
__ Garbage can
__ Toaster or toaster oven
__ Kettle
__ 1 four-quart pitcher
__ Cookbook
__ Eggbeater or hand mixer
__ Roasting pan with rack
__ Kitchen shears
__ Soup ladle
__ Dish drainer
__ Canister set for staples
__ 2 aprons, 1 full, 1 half-sized
__ 2–3 hot pads
__ 8–12 dish clothes
__ Tablecloth or place mats
__ Salt & pepper shakers
__ Paper towel dispenser
__ Napkin holder
__ Glassware
__ Flatware
__ Dinnerware

Kitchen Specialties

__ Cake pans
__ Pie plate
__ Jelly roll pan
__ Muffin tin
__ Cookie sheet
__ Sifter
__ Bean sprouter
__ Collapsible steamer basket
__ Pizza pan
__ Asparagus steamer
__ Cake decorating supplies
__ Rolling pin
__ Garlic press
__ Wok, electric or stove-top
__ Spice rack with spice variety
__ Glass 9"x13" baking dish
__ Marble pastry board
__ Glass covered cake plate
__ Pastry brush
__ Chopsticks
__ Cookie jar
__ Candy thermometer
__ Cookie cutters
__ Kabob Skewers

Kitchen Luxuries

__ Yogurt maker
__ Food processor
__ Bread mixer
__ Mini deep-fat fryer
__ Electric popcorn popper
__ Fondue pot
__ Noodle press
__ Microwave oven
__ Microwave cookware set
__ Juice extractor
__ Ice-cream maker
__ Hotdog cooker
__ Small pressure cooker
__ Hot plate
__ Salad shooter
__ Electric juicer
__ Peanut-butter maker
__ Electric frying pan
__ Crockpot
__ Food scale
__ Waffle iron

EMERGENCY CAR KITS

The following information has been assembled to help you organize emergency kits for your automobiles. It is a good idea to carry one in each car you own. Most of the items listed will be things you already have. There is an additional list for people that live in regions with cold and snowy winters. Cost is difficult to estimate, because it depends on what one might already have on hand. However, it is possible to spend $70–$100 if every item on the list has to be purchased.

MINI-CLASS IDEAS: This can be a great demonstration and can provide participation in a class setting. Many of these items are expensive if they each have to be purchased; however, the first aid kit is relatively inexpensive to assemble on a group basis. Take orders and collect money prior to the class. Purchase the items from a medical supply store in bulk for a better price. For the class, place the items on tables. Duplicate the Emergency Kit sheet to distribute as a handout. Instruct the participants to assemble their kits according to the lists provided on the handout (which also tells them how many of each item they need). Have them walk around the tables and pick up the items and place them in their kits. They can assemble the remainder of their Emergency Car Kits at home using their handouts as a guide.

EMERGENCY KITS

Basic Car Kit

__ Flashlight
__ Spare batteries
__ 3 emergency flares
__ Spare fuse kit
__ Fuse puller
__ Spare radiator hose
__ Jumper cables
__ Blanket or sleeping bag
__ Plastic poncho
__ Tire sealant and inflator
__ Adjustable wrench
__ Screwdrivers (Phillips & Standard)
__ Tire jack
__ First aid kit (see first aid kit list)
__ Light that plugs into cigarette lighter
__ Work gloves
__ Electrical wire (heavy gauge to lash a trunk or a loose tail pipe)
__ Duct tape
__ Spare fan belt
__ Pull-apart shovel
__ Bottled water
__ Canned food items and opener
__ Quart of engine oil
__ Chain or rope
__ Utility knife
__ Lug wrench

First Aid Kit

__ 10–12 adhesive bandages
__ 6 butterfly bandages
__ Two 4"x5" sterile conforming gauze bandages
__ Three extra-large adhesive bandages (2")
__ Three 3"x4" nonadhesive dressings
__ 2-3 sterile cotton tipped applicators
__ Neosporin antibiotic ointment
__ Six alcohol prep squares
__ Five cleansing towelettes in individual packages
__ One disposable instant ice compress
__ Antacid tablets
__ Aspirin or pain reliever tablets
__ Four wooden tongue depressors

Cold Winter Kit

__ Tire chains
__ Small bag of kitty litter (for tire traction)
__ Snow scraper
__ Matches or cigarette lighter
__ Winter gloves
__ Solar blanket
__ 2 cans "canned heat"
__ Aerosol deicer
__ Winter hat
__ Boots
__ Candle

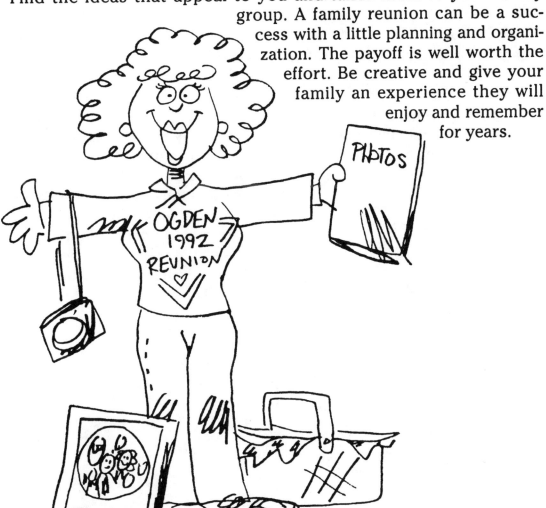

CREATIVE FAMILY REUNIONS

The challenge of hosting a family reunion can look terrifying, but with a few suggestions to help you plan your event, it can be a lot of fun. Find the ideas that appeal to you and tailor them to your family group. A family reunion can be a success with a little planning and organization. The payoff is well worth the effort. Be creative and give your family an experience they will enjoy and remember for years.

MINI-CLASS IDEAS: This can be an entertaining, "no cost" lecture. Duplicate Family Activity Ideas and Family Game and distribute as handouts at the beginning of the lecture. Touch on all suggestions and ask for others that your group may have to offer. At the end of the lecture take a few minutes to explain the *Family Game* and then play a couple of practice rounds.

Family Activities

1. *Family Newsletters* are often effective as you plan a reunion. They should include pertinent information and an agenda. You will find that the mail will be a cost efficient means of communication when working with large groups.

2. *Themes* are a lot of fun. They can be tied into the location of your reunion or just be chosen randomly. If you are camping near a famous landmark, provide information about it so everyone can learn something interesting. In the newsletter, suggest that everyone wear a specific color of shirt or bring their favorite hat to the reunion that ties in with the theme. Everyone doesn't have to match; just select a theme for them to follow.

3. *Family Auctions* are great fund-raisers. Some families have an auction in which they bid for items that are handmade by family members. This works best with large reunions; each individual family is required to make and donate something for the auction. The money is then used to pay for something special for the next year's reunion such as the meat for the picnic, reservations to a special show or campground, or the setting fee for a group photograph. Family Flea Markets where good usable items are brought to sell or trade can also be fun.

Family Reunion T-shirts are always fun. (Each member of the family should have one.)

- *Assign each family member to design their own shirt and then wear it at the reunion.*
- *Design a family T-shirt as a group project*
- *Have the shirts made at a local T-shirt shop for all the extended family*
- *Plan an activity in which every member decorates their own shirt with paints; then have everybody in the family sign each shirt.*

4. *Mystery Spotlights* on one family member can be another way to involve everyone in a reunion. Post the information about the individual and allow members to guess that person's identity. Or make a game of it by giving a clue to each person at the reunion and then giving them a chance to guess who the mystery person is. If they guess incorrectly, they forfeit the opportunity to guess again, and their clue is given to someone else. This can be especially fun for the children and for those of the second and third generations who may not be aware of some of the special experiences, talents, and accomplishments of family members.

5. *Name Tags* can be coded with numbers up to #3 to designate turns for the big meal of the reunion. All the #1's eat together then all the #2's eat together and the #3's last. This allows for maximum mingling and interaction. In large family gatherings you rarely know everyone there, and this random grouping helps everyone get acquainted or reacquainted.

6. *Family Group Pictures* are often taken at reunions. This requires extra planning and organization but is well worth the effort. Even *huge* groups can participate. It can be a great genealogy effort. (Remember how fun it was to see great-grandma's family picture?)

7. *Recipes* for favorite dishes that will be served at the family meal can be included in the newsletter so that everyone has them—those who will be preparing the food and those who will love eating it.

8. *Square Dancing* bridges generation gaps and provides fun for all participants. It also eliminates the awkwardness that some family members might feel. Records that include both the music and the voice of a caller are available at most libraries. You don't have to hire a professional caller.

9. *Games* including relay games, musical chairs, contests, and treasure hunts have remained my family's favorites. Road rallies with the group divided into teams, each with their own car and set of clues, have been another reunion success. The clues, usually written in riddle, tell the team where to find their next clue. The rally can take the participants all over town to familiar locations that can be easily recognized through the clues. There is a prize at the end of the race, and the first team to decipher all their clues, wins.

10. *Creative Games* will make family members more familiar with each other. You will find a copy of "the Family Game" at the end of this section. It's played like the "Newlywed" game and is a lot of fun. Be sure to mix the teams up (no spouses together) and try not to include close family members on the same team. Have paper and markers available so that the pairs can write their answers down, and be sure to include the question number on each answer sheet so that the proper response is held up for each question.

11. *Videotape* some of the activities. These tapes become priceless as family members move away, grow up, or pass away. It's also fun to look back and see how everyone changes from year to year. Use the same videotape each year, adding onto the end of the tape of each previous reunion so that it's all together.

12. *Videotape Life Histories* of some of the older members of the family. These are true treasures and are much easier to produce than transcriptions of speech. Of course, getting it down on paper is important for family records, but the ability to have the original story on tape and seeing the person talking are among the wonders of our day.

13. *Speakers* can be scheduled for classes or part of the reunion. Each year a different person can be asked to teach a class or speak on a topic. This is often of interest to adults only and the guest speaker may require a fee, but it can be a very nice part of a reunion. Choose topics of special interest or concern for your families such as genealogy, emergency preparedness, historical information, child rearing, family relations, or specific skills.

14. *Cultural Events* or special engagements can be a lot of fun. Most areas have plays, museums, or musical events available; tickets should be purchased in advance for those who want to attend. Parades, fairs, carnivals, trips to zoos, city tours, and civic festivals are also easy to incorporate into reunion activities. These are ideas that require input from all the families. They will also require a lot of planning, but the payoff can be worth the effort.

Helpful Hints

1. **Be sure you don't schedule every minute of the reunion.** Allow some free time for families and groups to do things that not everyone will want to participate in. This is important for families that are traveling significant distances in order to attend. They may want time to shop, tour scenic sites, or dine alone. They need the freedom to do so without guilt.

2. **Remember, the most successful newsletters are used to inform family members of events already planned.** Newsletters are usually not successful if they require families to respond in some way.

3. **Families will always have little ones who will want to participate.** Make sure to provide activities that are just for them. Fish ponds using donated toys and items are favorites. Face painting (clowns, Indians, animals), busy games such as "Red light—Green light" and "Red Rover," are great for children.

4. **Never underestimate the fun value of even the simplest activities.** Children and adults alike love to let their hair down; water fights, musical chairs, and silly games are just the ticket. Be sure that ground rules are laid down with things like water pistols, but don't exclude them just because they might get someone wet. You'd be surprised who will enjoy getting down and dirty. Capturing some of the fun with videos and cameras will make the memories last. These can be shared the following year so that everyone can enjoy them.

5. **Family reunions are for the unification and bonding of families.** They can be some of the best times you ever have. Strive to make them extra fun with as little forced effort as possible. Organization is the key to success, but don't be so organized and rigid that you miss the opportunities for growth and fun that spontaneity provides.

Instructions

1. Divide your group into teams of two (partner one and partner two). Give each team four sheets of paper and a marker. Send partner one of each partnership into another room, out of earshot. Read the first four game questions to partner two and have them write their answers on a separate piece of paper. It is helpful to have them number their answers so that they will respond correctly at the appropriate time. When they have completed their answers, make sure that the sheets of paper are arranged in order.

2. Have partner one return to the room. Read the same four questions, one at a time, to the returning partner, and have them give their answers verbally. After they have answered the first question, they can see the answer partner two wrote. The first correct answer is worth 5 points. Continue this process until all four questions are answered then tally the score. It is helpful to write the points on the back of the paper on which the answer for that question is written. That way, there won't be any confusion later. The second and third questions are each worth 5 points as well. The fourth question is worth 15 points.

3. When the teams have gone through the first four questions, send partner two into another room. Give partner one 4 blank sheets of paper to write their answers on. They need clean sheets to avoid mixing up the answers to any of the questions and in order to keep track of all the points.

4. Read the next four questions to partner one, which will be numbered 5–8. Have them write down their answers, just as their partner did before. When they have completed all their answers, partner two may return to the room to hear question 5, give their answer, and compare them to the response of partner one. Continue with question 6, 7 and 8. The scoring for this round of questions is the same as the first round, 5 points for questions 5, 6, and 7, and 15 points for question 8.

5. The third set of questions is to be handled the same as the first two, sending partner one out again. The remaining partner (partner two) is given 4 new sheets of paper, and the questions are read. The only part of this round that will be different is the scoring. Correct answers to questions 9, 10, and 11 are worth 10 points each, and question 12 is worth 20 points.

6. The fourth set of questions are handled the same as before. Partner two leaves the room and partner one answers the questions 13–16 on 4 new sheets of paper. When partner one has completed their answers, partner two returns to the room and gives his response to each question one at a time. Tally the scores: questions 13, 14, and 15 are worth 10 points each and question 16 is worth 15 points.

7. The bonus round will be the final 4 questions. Send partner one out again, hand out 4 new sheets of paper, and go through the last 4 question. Questions 17, 18, 19, and 20 are worth 15 points each. The final question is worth 25 points.

8. When partner one has returned, given their answers, and compared them to the responses of partner two, tally the points and determine the winning team. If a tie occurs, ask another question. The tiebreaker is question 21.

Family Game Questions

1. Which of the following best describes your partner?

    Donald Duck

    Godzilla

    The Stay-Puff Marshmallow Man

2. What is your partner's birthday?

3. Which of the following is your partner's least favorite?

    Baked beans

    Jelly beans

    Green beans

4. On the average, how many times a day does your partner open the refrigerator to find something to eat?

    3 times

    5 times

    8 times

5. What is your partner's favorite color?

6. Of Wendy's, Burger King, and McDonald's, which is your partners least favorite place to get a hamburger?

7. When was the last time your partner kissed a girl?

8. Does your partner prefer his eggs:

   Boiled

   Scrambled

   Staring back at him

9. Which of the following does your partner like best?

   Spiders

   Snakes

   Mice

10. When was the last time your partner rode a motorcycle?

13

11. Which of the following best describes the sound made when your partner blows his nose?

    A trumpet

    A leaking tire

    A vacuum cleaner sucking up a shirt

12. On the average, how many moles does your partner have?

    2

    20

    200

13. Which of the two of you will your partner say spends more time in the bathroom?

14. Which of the following ice cream flavors will your partner say best describes his personality?

    Rocky Road

    Nutty Coconut

    World Class Chocolate

15. Who will your partner say snores the most, you or him?

16. Which of the following does your partner need surgically removed from his body?

    A telephone

    A fork

    A television remote control

17. Complete this sentence to describe your partner:

    He who dies with the most_____, wins!

18. When was the last time your partner checked out a library book?

5 weeks

5 months

5 years

19. What vegetable will your partner say best describes his nose?

Potato

Carrot

Mushroom

20. Which will your partner say is his best physical feature?

21. (TieBreaker) Which of the following would best describe your partners sock drawer?

Gone with the Wind

Law and Order

Yours, Mine, and Ours

Arts & Crafts

STENCILING

Stenciling has been a method of decoration for centuries. Modern wallpaper began in an effort to mass-produce the effect of hand-stenciled walls and to make this type of decoration more affordable. Two hundred years ago, traveling artists worked door-to-door, beautifying colonial American homes. Their work has been documented and studied in some depth, and much of what they have done is still in existence. Today, it can add a special touch to your home, clothing, belongings, and gifts. Experiment with different stencils, and use them on different surfaces. Stenciling can be a wonderful expression of you, and it is a simple technique to master. See what you can dress up—you'll be amazed at what you can do!

MINI-CLASS IDEAS: Prior to the mini-class, provide participants with a list of materials they need to bring to the class. (Determine whether you will use precut stencils or make your own, and tailor the list accordingly.) Stencil on freezer paper taped to table tops. Display several different stenciled items to show the wide range of application, such as clothing, book bags, stationery, lamp shades, furniture, curtains, etc.

Approximate Cost: $5–$10

Needed Materials

- Acrylic paints coordinated with room
- Masking tape
- Yardstick
- Warm soapy water
- Makeup wedges or stencil brushes
- Precut stencils (or see below)

- Exact-o knife
- 10 or 12 gauge clear vinyl plastic (1/2 yd)
- Fine-tipped permanent marker

- Practice paper
- Scissors
- Palette
- Rags

- Stack of newspaper
- Pattern

Instructions

There are literally hundreds of pre-cut stencils to choose from these days, and they are wonderful for this project. However, making your own stencil is easy, and can tie together the decor of a room when there is a theme or a motif throughout. It should be noted that stenciling is not just for walls. Clothing, accessories, book covers, bedding, furniture, carpet, wood floors, stationery—almost anything—can be stenciled

If you choose to make your own stencil, follow these instructions:

Making a Stencil

1. Cut the clear vinyl into square sheets large enough to trace the entire pattern onto. (These squares should be the same size, and there should be one square for each color used in the stencil design.)

2. Trace the pattern you have selected onto each of the squares of vinyl required (one for each color). Trace the pattern in the same place on the vinyl for each stencil. Because each color has its own stencil, only portions of the total design will be cut from each stencil.

3. To cut the stencils out, place a single sheet of vinyl on the stack of newspapers.

—Using the Exact-o knife, cut along the design, turning the stencil around with your free hand.

—DO NOT lift the knife until the entire section is completely cut.

—Cut in long, continuous strokes and keep the knife moving in the same direction.

—Repeat for each square of vinyl.

—You are now ready to paint.

Painting & Printing

1. Before painting, practice first on a few sheets of paper.

2. Begin by centering your stencil on the paper and taping it into place. If you are using a makeup wedge to apply the paint, trim off any corners or angles from the sponge. Rounded edges blend the paint better than square ones.
It's easiest to have a separate sponge or brush for each color, but not absolutely necessary.

3. Stamp the sponge or brush up and down into the paint. When the sponge or brush is saturated, stamp most of the color out again on the newspaper.
(You want a very dry sponge or brush—an abundance of paint will seep under the stencil and smudge your design.)

4. Begin stenciling. Stenciling is done in a firm, up and down, pounding motion. The paint is pounded into the painted surface, using even pressure at all times. (Since your arm will tire when you paint walls, allow time for rest breaks.) When stenciling is done correctly, you will have more color around the edges of the cut-outs, and the color will fade as it moves toward the

center of each section. However, it is perfectly acceptable to stencil a solid section of color if that is what you prefer or what the design requires.

If paint seeps under your stencil, you are using too much paint. Remember to stamp most of the paint out of your sponges or brushes before using them on your project.

5. Repeat the above instructions for each color of your design.
You will be able to get the placement for each color right because you will have the entire design traced onto the vinyl sheet, even though only a portion has been cut out. Tape the stencil into place for each color. You don't want any movement of the stencil while you are painting.

6. After you feel confident that you are doing well on the practice paper, you are ready to move on to your project. If you are stenciling a border on your walls, be sure that the walls are clean and free of grease and dirt. The walls must have smooth, relatively untextured surface. Wood surfaces must be sealed prior to stenciling.

Paper does not require any previous preparation. Clothing, however, must be washed prior to painting. It is best to use "fabric medium" when painting on fabric. "Fabric medium" is mixed with the paint and helps it bond to the fabric fibers. It will not alter the color of the paint in any way, but it usually requires heat-setting after the paint has dried. The instructions on the product will help you if you are going to paint on fabrics. You can find "fabric medium" at craft or fabric stores.

7. Spacing is an important factor for stenciling. Measure the entire surface area to be stenciled, and divide this measurement by the size of the stencil pattern. (Be sure to include a space between the designs when measuring.) This will tell you how many repeats you can make. Mark your project accordingly. You do not have to end a pattern when you get to a corner. Your homemade stencils will wrap around a corner if you choose, or you can use the corners as breaks or spaces in your design. It is up to you.

Take your time and be creative. This is a skill you can use to personalize anything, easily, and inexpensively.

EMBOSSING WITH STENCILS

Have you noticed how much a single greeting card costs these days? For the price of a stencil (usually less than a greeting card), you can make beautiful, personal cards and stationery. The stencil can be used over and over (unlike a purchased card), and the technique is easy enough for your children to learn. Discover how much fun it can be to design your own greeting cards, gift tags, stationery, and note cards!

MINI-CLASS IDEAS: This mini-class requires a little preparation. Make several different samples for display. Emboss stationery, place cards, gift tags, and greeting cards. Show examples of indented embossing as well as the raised type. Make arrangements to have a glass topped table and a lamp for use, or you can use glass windows if your class is taught during daylight hours. Have each of the participants bring their own stencils. Find a ceramic store that will let you purchase several styluses and return any you don't need. Provide a few sheets of 20# paper for each participant.

Approximate Cost: $5

Needed Materials

- Commercial Stencils
- Fine-point permanent marker (black)
- Stylus
- Colored 20# paper
- Large piece of glass
- Light source
- Masking tape

Instructions

1. The key to embossing is a good light table or a glass window during daylight hours. Glass topped tables are also excellent. Or if you have a table that has removable leaves, place the leaves 8"-10" apart and place a piece of glass from a picture frame over the hole. Set a lamp under the table below the glass, and you have a light table. If you use a piece of glass from a picture frame, tape the edges with masking or strapping tape so that you will not get cut.

2. The second part of successful embossing is to use the proper paper. Paper is identified by its weight. The best weight is 20# (20 pound) paper, found at any copy shop and available in a rainbow of colors.

3. Choose a stylus. Many people do not know what a stylus is. It is a tool used in cleaning ceramic greenware or in Tole painting. It looks like a pencil that has a needle in one end tipped with a round metal ball. It can be found in craft or ceramic shops. The round ball at the end must be at least as large as a ball in a ball point pen. If the ball is too small, it punctures the paper and ruins your piece. The best type of stylus has metal ends on each side and two different size balls to choose from.

4. Now choose your stencil. Any commercial stencil that is cut from thin plastic will work. The stencil must have some degree of thickness to be effective because it is the depth of the cuts that makes your raised image.

5. Trace around the edges of all stencil images on the back side of your stencil with a black permanent marker. (Tracing on the back side of the stencils insures that no ink will come off on your pieces while you work.)

6. When embossing, work from the inside, or wrong side, just as you do when sewing. Place your stencil on the glass of your light source with permanent markings facing the glass. If you are using a window, you can tape the stencil to the glass so that it stays up while you work. If you are making a folded card, fold the paper, and place it right side down on the stencil. Otherwise, position your paper as desired, remembering to place the right side down on the stencil. The tracings around the stencil cuts can be seen through your paper so that you can position the stencil exactly where you want it. With your stylus, trace around the image of the stencil. As you move around the pattern, the stylus forces the paper down along the edges of the cuts in the stencil and creates a raised image in the paper.

7. Turn your paper over to see the embossed image. Mix and match stencil patterns, or reverse the embossing to make some of the images raised and others indented.

Possible Stencil Patterns

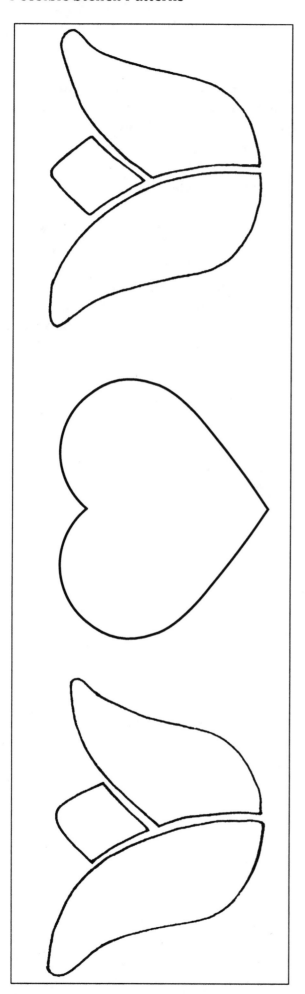
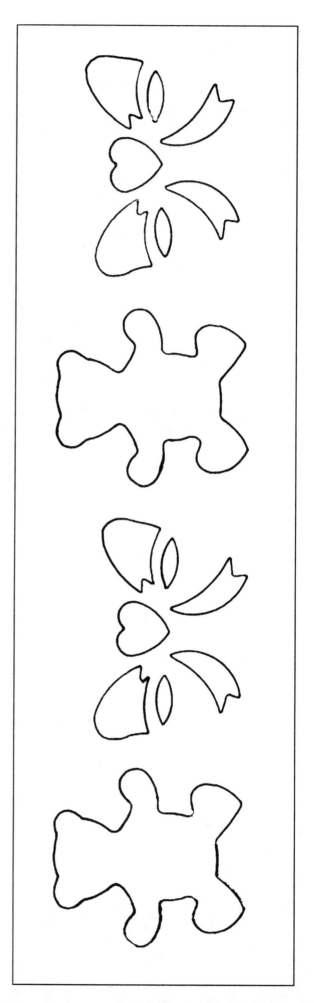

CREATIVE TWIST BASKET

This basket is an easy, impressive little project with endless possibilities. It can be filled with flowers for your home, homemade goodies for a sick friend, eggs and candy for Easter . . . you decide! The cost is minimal, the time worthwhile.

MINI-CLASS IDEAS:
Provide a list of materials required prior to class. Provide tables to work on with access to electrical outlets for the hot glue guns.

Approximate Cost: $2–$5

Needed Materials

- 12 yards Creative Twist paper, for single color basket,
  12 yards (6 yards of each color) for 2 color basket
- Hot glue gun & glue sticks
- Scissors
- Yardstick
- 26 gauge wire
- Wire cutters

These baskets have unlimited potential, year round. They can make wonderful Easter baskets, gift baskets, holiday decorations (how about red-white-and blue for July?), and accents in your home. With the tremendous variety in Creative Twist colors, the sky is the limit.

Instructions:

1. To begin, cut 10 pieces of Creative Twist paper, each 18" long. Untwist the pieces completely and fold them into thirds lengthwise, so that each piece is 18" long and $\frac{1}{3}$ the width of the original piece. Set aside.

2. Next, cut 5 pieces, each 28" long. If you are making a dual colored basket, cut 3 pieces in an accent color, and 2 more pieces in the first color (these two pieces will make the braided handle). Untwist all 5 pieces completely. Cut the 2 handle pieces in half width-wise so that there are 4 pieces that are half the original width and 28" long. Set aside. Fold the remaining 3 pieces in thirds lengthwise, as with the 10 pieces in step one. Set the leftover piece of twisted paper aside to make the finishing strip.

3. The bottom of the basket is woven first. Run five 18" pieces horizontally and five 18" pieces vertically. Lay 5 folded pieces down on a flat surface in front of you, side by side, vertically. Begin weaving the horizontal pieces through the vertical pieces, starting $4\frac{1}{2}$" down from the top of the vertical pieces, and leaving $4\frac{1}{2}$" on each side of the horizontal pieces. Weave this center portion tightly, placing each horizontal piece right up next to the piece previously woven. Refer to diagram A for clarification.

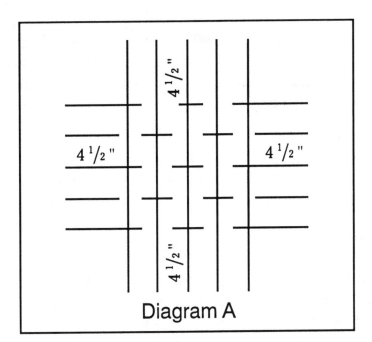

Diagram A

4. After you have woven the 5 horizontal pieces into the center of the 5 vertical pieces, fold each 4^1/$_2$" end over toward the center. This creases the paper and helps it stand up to create the sides of the basket. When each piece has been folded over on both ends, prepare the wire form.

5. Make a square wire form measuring 6" per side using 4 strands of 26 gauge floral wire. If your wire is shorter than the 26"-28" length necessary, twist two lengths of 4 strands each together, and make the form. Trim away any excess.

6. Attach the form to the inside of the basket. Stand a 4^1/$_2$" end up, bending at the crease made in step 4, and fold the top ^{1}/$_2$" over, toward the inside of the basket, with the form situated under the ^{1}/$_2$" fold. Make sure the corners of the wire form are placed at the corners of the basket. Glue the top ^{1}/$_2$" fold into place with hot glue. You may need to hold the paper in place until the hot glue sets. Repeat this step all the way around the basket to form the basket sides. When this is completed, you are ready to weave the twisted paper through the sides of the basket.

7. Begin at the bottom in the *middle* of any side. Weave the first of 3 rows around the bottom of the basket, overlap the ends when the weaving is complete and the hot glue in place. Weave the second or middle row around the sides of the basket. Weave this piece as close

31

to the first row as you can so that there are as few gaps between woven rows as possible. Overlap and glue into place, holding if necessary while the glue sets. Now weave the third and final row tightly against the second row, overlap, and glue into place as you did with the previous two rows. If this is a dual colored basket, these pieces will be different colors.

8. Braid the handle from three of the four pieces that were set aside for this purpose. These pieces are folded into thirds lengthwise, and braided down their length. A good length for the braided handle is 18–20 inches. Trim off excess *after* braiding. Hot glue each end into place in the center of any two opposite basket sides.

9. Fold the fourth 28" piece, leftover from the handle pieces, into thirds, lengthwise. Hot glue this piece around the inside of the basket over the folded ends at the top of the basket sides and over the handle attachments. This finishes the inside of the basket.

10. Untwist the leftover twisted paper and make a bow, securing it in the middle with a piece of 26 gauge wire folded in half. Attach the bow to the basket with the ends of this wire, placing it wherever you choose.

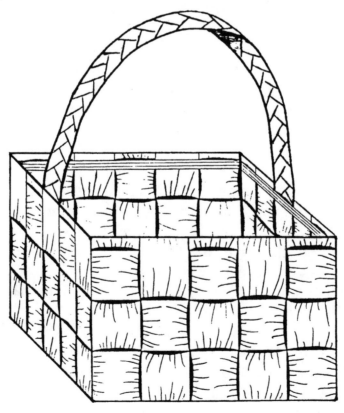

Cooking

DELICIOUS NUTRITIOUS DRINKS

These recipes are for those of us that find it all too easy to skip meals. These drinks contain proteins and fruits, providing vital nutrients to keep you going through the day. You will find these drinks will be great for breakfast, but they can be enjoyed any time of the day.

MINI-CLASS IDEAS: This is a great demonstration class. Provide the recipes as a handout, and prepare each drink while participants watch. Make enough for all to sample each drink.

Grape Gulps

2 1/2 cups grape juice
1 1/2 cups vanilla yogurt
4 eggs
1/2 tsp. vanilla extract

Combine ingredients in
blender. Blend until
smooth.
Makes 4 servings.

NOTES:

Strawberry Smoothie

1 3/4 cups cranberry juice
1 cup cottage cheese
1 cup packed frozen strawberries
2 eggs
1 1/2 tsp. vanilla extract
2 tsp. sugar

Combine ingredients in blender. Blend until smooth.
Makes 3 servings.

NOTES:

Egg Delight

4 cups milk
2 cups vanilla ice cream
6 eggs
3 Tbsp. honey
2 Tbsp. wheat germ
$1/4$ tsp. ground nutmeg
$1/2$ tsp. vanilla extract

Combine ingredients in blender. Blend until smooth.
Makes 6 servings.

NOTES:

Peachy Cream Shake

1 cup peach slices (canned, or fresh and peeled)
$1/2$ cup milk
$2/3$ cup vanilla yogurt
1 tsp. vanilla extract
2 eggs
1 Tbsp. brown sugar

Combine ingredients in blender.
Blend until smooth. Makes 2 servings.

NOTES:

Banana Bang

3 ripe bananas, peeled and sliced
3 cups pineapple juice
2 cups lemon sherbet
3 eggs
1 cup crushed ice

Combine ingredients in blender.
Blend until smooth. Makes 6 servings.

NOTES:

Orange-Apricot Chiller

Two 12-oz. cans apricot nectar
One 6-oz. can frozen orange juice concentrate
$\frac{1}{8}$ tsp. ground cloves
$\frac{1}{8}$ tsp. cinnamon
$\frac{1}{8}$ tsp. nutmeg
3 eggs

Combine ingredients in blender. Blend until smooth.
Makes 3 servings.

NOTES:

WORKING MOTHER'S BREAKFASTS

These wonderful recipes are designed for those of us who find that making breakfast for ourselves or our families can be the greatest challenge of the day. Each was planned with taste, time, and health in mind. Breakfast *can* be the most delicious meal of the day without being the most hassle.

MINI-CLASS IDEAS: This is another great demonstration class. Have each recipe prepared by a different person prior to class. Allow each cook time to discuss the recipe they used and have them give tips for preparation. Pass around samples of the fare and send each participant home with a handout and a smile!

YOGURT BREAKFAST POPS

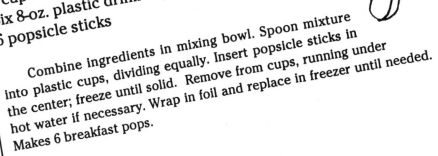

One 24-oz. container vanilla yogurt
4 small bananas, sliced
1¹/₂ cups sliced strawberries
1 cup miniature marshmallows
Six 8-oz. plastic drink cups
6 popsicle sticks

Combine ingredients in mixing bowl. Spoon mixture into plastic cups, dividing equally. Insert popsicle sticks in the center; freeze until solid. Remove from cups, running under hot water if necessary. Wrap in foil and replace in freezer until needed. Makes 6 breakfast pops.

NOTES:

BANANA BREAKFAST SHAKE

3 ripe bananas, peeled and sliced
2 cups lemon sherbet
3 cups unsweetened grapefruit juice
2 eggs
1¹/₂ cup crushed ice
¹/₂ tsp. vanilla

In a blender, combine all ingredients. Blend until smooth. Makes 6 servings.

NOTES:

REFRIGERATOR MUFFINS

Make the batter and store in a large covered container. Bake in paper muffin cups as you need them. The batter will keep for up to 3 months!

2 cups oatmeal
2 cups (3 large bars) shredded wheat
2 cups boiling water
4 beaten eggs
5 tsp. soda
3 tsp. cinnamon
1 quart buttermilk
2 cups coarsely chopped walnuts

2 cups all-bran cereal
1 cup shortening
1 $^3/_4$ cup sugar
5 cups flour
1 tsp. salt
1 tsp. cloves
2 cups raisins

In extra large mixing bowl, mix cereals together and pour boiling water over them. In different bowl, cream shortening, eggs, and sugar; add to cereal mixture in large bowl. Mix dry ingredients together and sift into big bowl with buttermilk. Stir in raisins and nuts. Bake 12-20 minutes at 425 degrees in greased or paper lined muffin tins. Makes 30-40 muffins.

BACON-CHEESE BREAKFAST PIE

One 9-in. unbaked pastry shell
$^1/_2$ cup chopped onion
1 Tbsp. dried parsley flakes
1 4-oz. can sliced mushrooms, drained
1 cup (4 oz.) shredded cheddar cheese
1 cup (4 oz.) shredded Swiss cheese

$^1/_2$ lb. bacon
4 eggs
$^1/_4$ tsp. pepper
$^1/_2$ tsp. salt
1 $^3/_4$ cups milk
2 cups dried beans

Preheat oven to 425°. Line bottom of the unbaked shell with foil and fill with dried beans to keep pastry flat while baking. Bake for 7 minutes. Remove from oven. Remove foil and beans and cool.

Fry bacon in skillet until crisp. Remove, drain on paper towel, then crumble. Set aside. Sauté onions in bacon drippings until tender. Remove from heat and add to bacon.

In a large bowl, beat eggs. Add milk, salt, pepper, parsley. Stir in bacon, onions, mushrooms, and cheese. Carefully pour into prebaked pie shell; do not splash onto sides of pastry shell.

Bake 15 minutes. Reduce temperature to 350° and bake an additional 30 minutes. Cool completely. Cut into 6 slices, carefully wrap individually in foil, and freeze. Warm in microwave for 2 minutes before eating. Makes 6 servings.

BREAKFAST CASSEROLE

1 loaf French bread
$^1/_2$ lb. grated cheddar cheese
$^1/_2$ tsp. dried mustard
1 lb. bacon or ground sausage
$^3/_4$ cup chopped onion
2 cups milk
6 eggs
$^1/_4$ tsp. pepper
$^1/_2$ tsp. salt

Slice French bread in half lengthwise, then cube. Line the bottom of buttered 9"x12" cake pan. In a skillet, fry meat then drain off all but 1 Tbsp. of drippings. Drain meat on paper towel, crumble meat and set aside. Sauté onions until tender in 1 Tbsp. of drippings. Remove from heat, add to meat, and sprinkle both over bread.

In medium mixing bowl, beat eggs. Add dried mustard, salt, and pepper. Carefully pour over the meat-covered bread. Sprinkle grated cheese over everything, and cover the pan with foil. Let stand in refrigerator for 24 hours. Remove foil, bake for 45 minutes at 350 degrees. Garnish with fresh fruit and parsley sprig. Makes 9-12 servings.

FRUIT & CHEESE PITA BREAKFAST

6–8 pita pockets
Two 4-oz. containers of vanilla yogurt
$^1/_2$ cup shredded coconut
4 small bananas, peeled and sliced
1 small can mandarin oranges
$^1/_3$ cup unsalted sunflower seeds or coarsely chopped walnuts
1 cup grated cheddar cheese

In blender, pour yogurt and cheese; process until smooth. Mix remaining ingredients in medium mixing bowl; add yogurt-cheese mixture. Stir thoroughly. Spoon into pita pockets. Pin pockets together with round toothpicks. Wrap individually in foil and freeze. Place in refrigerator overnight to thaw for breakfast. Makes 6–8 servings.

NOTES:

NO-MACHINE ICE CREAMS

This is the section that's perfect for those of us who don't have an ice-cream freezer but love the flavor of fresh, homemade ice cream. It's made from a meringue base and flavored with your favorite pureed fruit.

MINI-CLASS IDEAS: This can be a very successful demonstration. Have several people prepare different flavors of ice cream prior to class. Serve some flavors for samples. Allow each person time to discuss the recipe they used and to give tips for preparation. Allow participants to sample each flavor and take home the recipes. It may be helpful to bring a prepared meringue base to show to the participants.

MERINGUE BASE FOR FRUIT-FLAVORED ICE CREAMS

$^1/_4$ cup water
$^1/_8$ tsp. cream of tartar

$^1/_2$ cup sugar
2 egg whites

—In heavy saucepan, combine sugar and water. Bring to a boil over high heat and continue boiling to soft ball stage, or 240 degrees on a candy thermometer. In a small mixing bowl, beat egg whites and cream of tartar until stiff peaks are formed. Continue beating at high speed, gradually adding the hot syrup in a thin stream, until very stiff. (This takes approximately 5 minutes.) Remove, place in large bowl, and cool in refrigerator for 20 minutes. The meringue is ready for fruit puree and cream. However, if it becomes too stiff to add the puree, simply beat with wire whisk till softened. Makes approx. 1 $^1/_2$ quarts of ice cream.

—Requires about 8 hours to freeze. Best to freeze in stainless steel, glass, or ceramic bowls.

BASIC INSTRUCTIONS FOR FRUIT AND CREAM FLAVORS

Place the fruits, flavors, and sugar in a blender and process on high until smooth. Scrape puree into a mixing bowl, cover, and cool in refrigerator. Prepare the cream in a separate bowl by beating at a high speed until it becomes stiff. Fold gently into the cooled, prepared meringue base. Spoon the puree onto the meringue and carefully fold until combined completely. Freeze in recommended container for 8 hours for ice cream or serve partially softened as a parfait.

ORANGE DELIGHT

1 1/2 Tbsp. grated orange rind
1/3 cup fresh orange juice
1/4 cup sugar
1 cup heavy cream
Prepared meringue base— See page 44

Follow basic instructions to prepare. This is a wonderful flavor to serve partially chilled as a parfait layered with crushed vanilla wafers and topped with a dollop of cream.

NOTES:

PINEAPPLE-STRAWBERRY MARBLE MARVEL

1 1/2 cups strawberries, topped and sliced
1 1/2 cups fresh pineapple, cubed
6 Tbsp. sugar
1 cup heavy cream
Prepared meringue base— See page 44

Follow basic instructions to prepare. However, each fruit is pureed separately; after the cream is folded into the meringue base, it is divided in half. Each fruit is folded into one half, as outlined above and then spooned alternately into a 1 1/2 quart bowl. Marble with knife, lay plastic wrap on the surface to retain swirls as it freezes, and serve when firm.

NOTES:

TROPICAL TREAT

1/4 cup fresh lime juice
2 cups ripe red or green mangoes, peeled, pitted, sliced
1 large ripe banana, peeled, sliced
1/4 cup sugar
1 cup heavy cream
2 tsp. pineapple extract
Prepared meringue base—See page 44

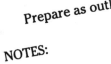

Prepare as outlined in basic instructions.

NOTES:

APPLE-CINNAMON CRUNCH CREAM

2 cups prepared applesauce
1/4 cup sugar
1 tsp. ground cinnamon
1/4 tsp. ground cloves
1/2 tsp. nutmeg
1 cup heavy cream
Prepared meringue base—See page 44

Prepare as outlined in basic instructions. Serve partially thawed as a parfait layered with granola.

NOTES:

REMARKABLE RASPBERRY-BANANA ICE CREAM

2 cups raspberries
1/2 cup water
1/3 cup sugar
1 large ripe banana, sliced
1 cup heavy cream
Prepared meringue base—See page 44

Combine berries, water, and sugar in saucepan. Bring to boil. Simmer for 20 minutes at reduced heat. Press berry mixture through sieve to remove seeds. Pour strained fruit juice into blender, add banana slices, process until smooth. Cover and chill. Finish recipe as outlined in basic instructions above.

PEACHES 'N ICE CREAM

3 cups peaches, peeled, pitted, sliced (approx. 5 peaches)
2 Tbsp. lemon juice
1/3 cup sugar
1/2 tsp. almond extract
1 cup heavy cream
Prepared meringue base—See page 44

Prepare as outlined above in basic instructions.

NOTES:

Sewing

HEIRLOOM HANGERS

These lovely hangers are reminiscent of the elegance and beauty of the Victorian era. They can be used to hang or display special items such as baby blessing dresses, or can be added to a bride's trousseau. With lavish embellishments of lace and ribbon, pearls and flowers, these hangers will be treasured gifts, or favorite show pieces.

MINI-CLASS IDEAS: Prior to the class, provide a list of materials that each participant must bring—including their own sewing machines. This project will require a large work area with tables and access to several electrical outlets. Two or three irons and ironing boards will also be required. Patterns should be prepared and ready for each participant to use at the beginning of class. This project can be completed in approximately 45 minutes.

Approximate Cost: $3–$8

Needed Materials

- $^1/_2$ yd. bridal satin, white or ivory
- 2 Wire hangers
- $^1/_2$" quilt batting, 45" x 18"
- Yarn, white or ivory, to match fabric
- Coordinating thread
- Scissors
- Straight pins
- Sewing needle
- Assorted trims, lace, and beads
- 1 yard braided trim, white or ivory to match fabric
- Hot glue gun

These materials will make one pair of heirloom hangers.

Instructions

1. Wrap the hook of the hanger tightly with yarn, securing at each end with hot glue. According to the pattern included, cut 4 pieces of bridal satin and 4 pieces of quilt batting. Set the satin aside.

2. Lay the hanger between two pieces of batting and whip-stitch the front and back pieces together along all sides of the hanger. Trim the excess from the bottom before stitching it around the hanger. When hangers are "upholstered," set aside.

3. With right sides together, stitch satin starting at the bottom and moving up the angled sides of the hanger cover with a $^3/_8$" seam; leave an opening at the center top to insert the hanger through. Clip curves.

4. Fold each bottom straight edge up $^1/_2$" and hem. Turn right sides out and press.

5. Slip the hanger cover over the hanger and pin the bottom closed, snug along the hanger. With a zipper foot, stitch the bottom shut with the seam snug with the hanger bottom. With a zipper foot, attach a length of lavish lace on the front side at the bottom of the hanger. Gather lavish lace for the top with a basting stitch so the fullness will lay nicely across the top of the hanger, and glue around

the neck of the hanger with the hot glue gun. Stitch or glue ribbons, beads, flowers, etc. to trim the front of the hanger. On the back, hot glue braided trim over the seam lines at the bottom of the hanger, turning ends under to finish.

6. These beautiful hangers can be displayed and enjoyed on their own merits or used to hang favorite clothing items. Try slipping potpourri between the layers of batting before whip-stitching shut for a delicate fragrance. These can be given as gifts or treasured for yourself as replicas of heirlooms from days gone by.

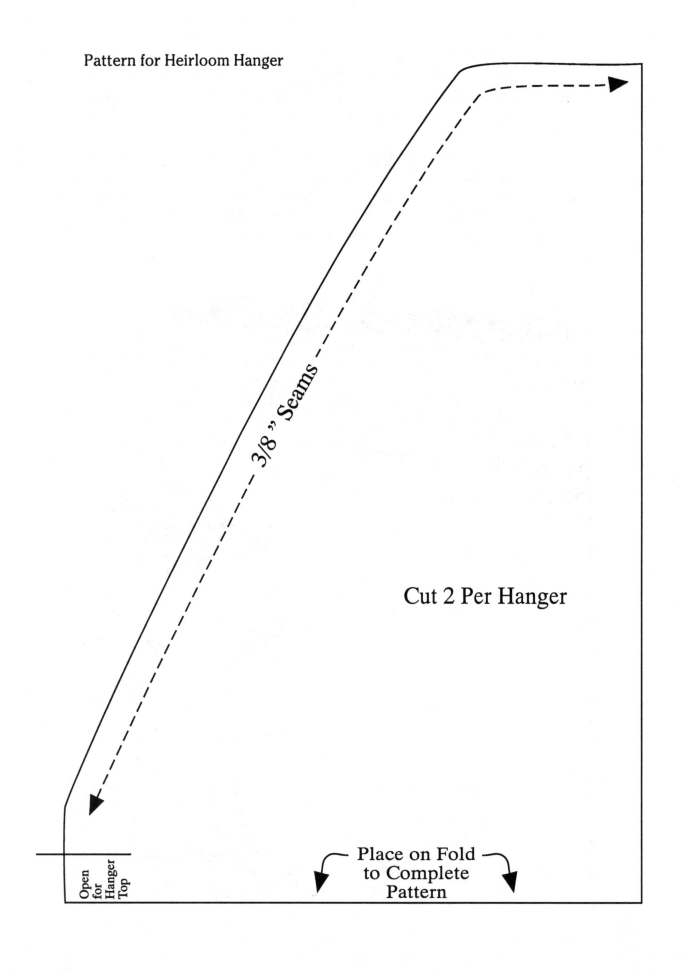

Pattern for Heirloom Hanger

3/8 " Seams

Cut 2 Per Hanger

Open for Hanger Top

Place on Fold to Complete Pattern

CHILD'S CARD TABLE TENT

This delightful project is made to fit over any square, folding card table. It can be made in a few hours and can provide years of fun and enjoyment.

MINI-CLASS IDEAS: Prior to the class, provide each participant with a list of materials she must bring. Each participant should bring her own sewing machine. This project will require a large work area with tables and access to several electrical outlets. Two or three irons and ironing boards will also be required. If participants wish to use appliques, the project will take considerably longer to complete. It may be wise to have them applique their panels prior to class. Sergers are wonderful for this project. It is easier if one person purchases the clear plastic vinyl for all participants and then divides it among the group, since the vinyl is sometimes difficult to find and there is waste if each person purchases her own. This project can be completed in approximately one hour if no appliques are used.

SEWING

Approximate Cost: $10–$25

Needed Materials

- 5 yards cotton or cotton blend fabric, may be printed or solid
- 10-gauge clear plastic vinyl, approx. 24" x 14" long
- Iron
- Coordinating thread
- Scissors
- Straight pins
- Juvenile pillow panels (optional)
- Measuring tape
- Wonder Under (optional)
- Chalk

Instructions

1. Measure your card table. You will need dimensions for the table-tops, and the sides. Most square card table are approx. 35" by 35" by 27". When you have the exact measurements, add 1" to the width and the length of the tabletop for $1/2$" seam allowances. Add 1" to the width and 2" to the length measurements of the side panels for seam allowances and rolled hem.

2. With new measurements, cut one piece of fabric for your tabletop, and one for each side.

Most card tabletops have rounded corners, and you will need to alter your fabric corners for the tabletop. To do so, place the square piece of fabric on the tabletop, and adjust it so that the $1/2$" seam allowances are even around all sides. Trace around the corner configurations with a piece of chalk. Add $1/2$" to the new configurations for the seam allowances at the corners and cut.

For patterned fabric: If you have selected a printed fabric for your tent, you will probably want to add only a clear plastic window.

For solid fabric: When using a solid colored fabric it is often fun to applique juvenile printed pillow panels onto some of the sides, or even on the inside of the tent. You will also want to include a clear plastic window. If you choose to applique the pillow panels onto the sides of the tent, it should be done at this point. To do this, press

Wonder Under onto the back sides of the printed pattern. Cut around the outline of the character, remove the paper backing from the Wonder Under, and press with a hot iron. Using a zigzag stitch, sew around the character.

3. To attach the window to the tent, cut the plastic, making sure it is squared.

Place the plastic in the center of a side piece of fabric, pin in place at the four corners, and zig-zag into place. Turn the piece of fabric over, and trim away all but $1/4$" of the fabric behind the plastic window.

4. When the window and any appliques have been attached, sew the 4 side pieces together lengthwise, forming a single length of fabric. This is done by joining the side pieces, right sides together, one at a time, adding onto the previously seamed side piece.

Finish each seam with a narrow zigzag stitch to prevent unraveling and early deterioration.

5. Sew the two remaining ends which are unseamed in a narrow rolled hem to form the opening of the tent. Stitch the rolled hem at the bottom of the continuous length of fabric.

6. When the hem is completed, press the entire piece with an iron.

7. Using straight pins, attach the sides to the top of the tent.

With right sides together, begin at one corner of the top piece and pin an end (with a rolled hem) to the center of the rounded corner. Move on to the next corner and pin the next seamed corner of the side piece to the center of the rounded corner. Continue until you are back at the first corner. Then pin the last end next to the first end you started with. Now go back and pin the fabric more thoroughly between the corners (some easing may be necessary). See Diagram A on next page.

8. When the sides are all pinned to the top of the tent, sew with a $1/2$" seam allowance. To complete your project, finish the seam edges with a narrow zigzag stitch.

Table Tent Diagram A

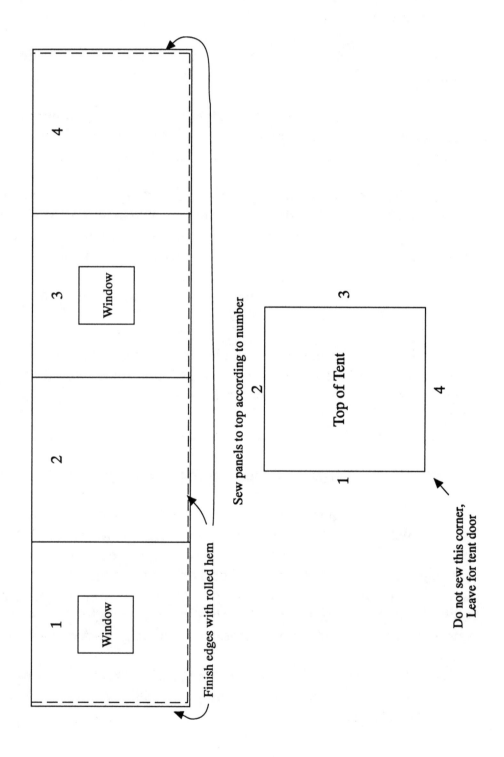

CROSS-STITCH WELCOME MATS

This popular project will give any door a warm and welcome touch. Using simple skills, this is an easy way to add your personal flair. Make one for each holiday (using glow-in-the-dark fabric for Halloween), or give them as gifts. These are simple enough for older children to make and it's a great way to use those fabric scraps you have been collecting for years. You can even design your own patterns with graph paper and a little imagination.

MINI-CLASS IDEAS: This project is most successful if the following suggestions are carried out: Have one person purchase the sea grass mats so they will all be identical, and participants can take advantage of a bulk-rate discount. Select one pattern and duplicate for each participant the pattern and the list of materials needed. Be sure the pattern you select will fit into the parameters of the mats. Everyone should work on the same pattern for the demonstration. They should have their fabric prewashed and torn into strips. This needs to be done prior to class. Cross-stitch is an easy skill, and a simple pattern can be completed in about an hour if the above steps are followed.

Approx. Cost: $1–$8
(Price varies with fabrics and patterns selected. Scraps that you have around the house are perfectly suitable.)

Needed Materials

- One 24 $\frac{1}{2}$" x 14 $\frac{1}{2}$" woven sea grass mat
- Solid broadcloth-weight fabric, 45" wide (100% cotton recommended)
- Size 14 tapestry needle
- Masking tape
- Cross-stitch pattern of your choice*
- Ruler
- Scissors

Note: The fabric selected should match the recommended embroidery floss colors of the pattern as closely as possible. Don't rule out prints; they can give a fun look to your mat.

*The pattern selected cannot be more than 30 stitches wide and 16 stitches long, since that is all the parameters of the mat will allow. It's also a good idea to choose a pattern that has 5 colors or less.

Instructions

1. Fabric must be prewashed and dried prior to beginning this project.

2. Tear prewashed fabric, selvage-to-selvage, into 1$\frac{1}{2}$" strips. These strips will make 6–8 stitches each. To determine how many strips to tear, count the number of stitches to be made in each color, according to the pattern, and divide by 7. Half a yard of fabric will yield 12 strips and 84 stitches.

3. Find the center knot in mat. Mark with masking tape. Work from the center of your pattern to avoid slight variations in the mats.

Lay out cross-stitch patterns on a grid. Each square represents a single stitch. Some patterns have colored instructional diagrams and symbols, and some are black and white and use separate symbols to represent the different colors used in the pattern. Back-stitch lines, or the outlines of the pattern, are usually indicated by straight lines. You will not back-stitch on this mat. See your pattern instructions for any special information.

5. On cross-stitch canvas, a stitch is normally made from corner to corner in the small squares found on the canvas (usually called Aida cloth). On the grass mat make a stitch over each knot of the mat, from corner to corner of each individual square of the mat. Fold the fabric strips in half lengthwise, and thread each one through the eye of the tapestry needle. Complete each cross-stitch individually, starting from the bottom left corner of a square and move diagonally to the top right corner; then take the stitch under the mat down to the bottom right corner of the square and move diagonally up to the top left corner to make a complete "X," Bring the needle from the back up through the center of the small holes at each corner of the knots. Make a 3" tail before beginning the first stitch. After the 6–8 stitches are made, run the needle under the stitches on the back of the mat, and pull the needle off of strip end. Work the tail from the beginning of the strip into stitches on the back of the mat. Begin and end each additional strip by running the needle under several stitches on the back. Do not tie knots.

6. You can clean these mats with Windex and a stiff bristled cleaning brush.

Possible Cross-Stitch Welcome Mat Patterns

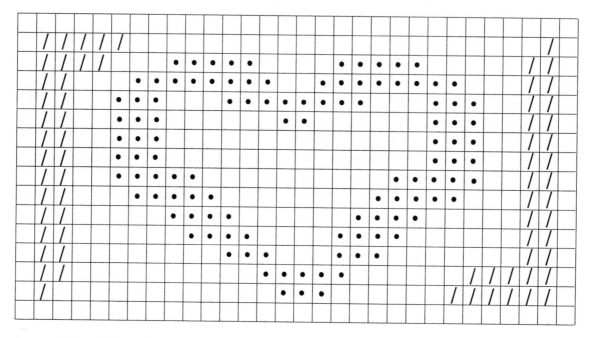

Cross-Stitch Heart Key: • Red,   / White

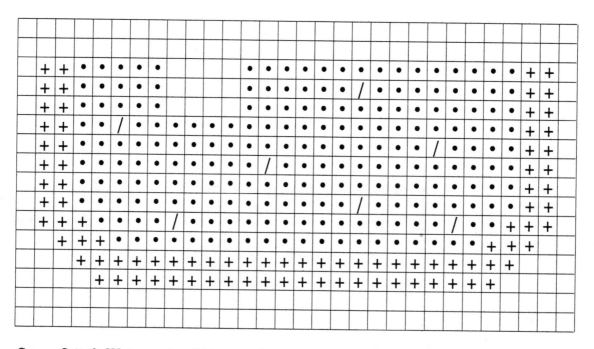

Cross-Stitch Watermelon Key: + Green, • Red, / Black

Possible Cross-Stitch Welcome Mat Patterns

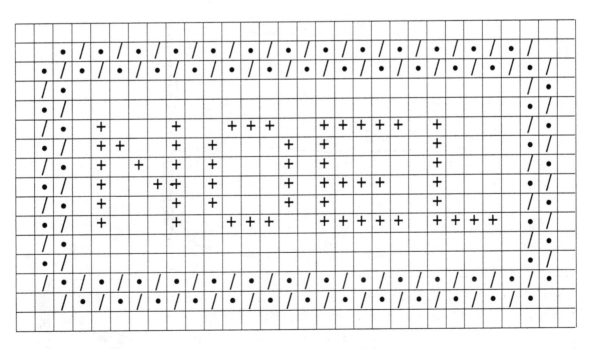

Cross-Stitch Welcome Key: X Blue,   • Pink

Cross-Stitch Noel Key: + Green,   • Red,   / White

CAR TRAVEL CADDYS

This is a great little item that you can make to hold your children's toys or the things that are always rolling around in your car (windshield scrapers, flashlights, tissues, maps, pens, etc.). It can be made from scraps of fabric or you can purchase the fabric required. After it is ready for your car, simply fasten it to the backs of the front seats. Every car should have at least one. Two are great if you are likely to have more than one child buckled in the back seat.

MINI-CLASS IDEAS: Provide a list of materials required prior to the class. Each participant should bring her own sewing machine. This project will require a large work area with tables and access to several electrical outlets. Two or three irons and ironing boards will also be needed.

Approximate Cost: $0–$10 (Price subject to fabric selected)

Needed Materials

- 1 yard denim or other heavy-duty fabric
- Thread
- Iron
- Chalk
- Pattern (included on next page)

- Scissors
- Heavy duty sewing needle
- Yardstick
- Straight pins

Instructions

Fabric must be prewashed prior to beginning this project.

1. Lay prewashed fabric open flat on the floor or a large work area. It may be necessary to press the fabric after it is prewashed because some fabric will be very wrinkled. Using the yardstick and chalk, mark the pattern on the fabric as indicated on the pattern below:

2. Cut the strips of fabric out carefully in straight, even pieces. With the chalk and yardstick, mark the dotted pocket placement lines on the front piece of the caddy (see finished diagram on page 59). Next, mark a vertical line dividing two of the pockets (the top and middle pockets) down the middle.

3. All seams in this project will be $^5/_8$".

4. Fold the 4 strap pieces in half lengthwise, with right sides together. Stitch one end and the long side, leaving one end open. Trim the seam allowances

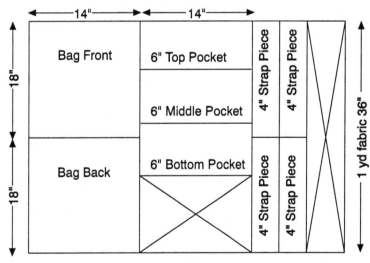

at the corners. Turn the straps right side out, and press. Sew the Velcro strips to the seamed ends so that they will overlap when fastened. This means one strap will have Velcro on the top side and one strap will have Velcro on the bottom side. Set aside.

5. Lay all of the pocket pieces down, wrong side up. Make a narrow, double-rolled hem at the top of each of the 3 pocket pieces; stitch and press the hems. Lay the two top pockets (the ones divided in half with chalk) on the right side of the front piece, *right sides together,* with the unfinished bottoms of the pockets lined up with the markings on the front piece. Stitch them in place. Press the seams open. Bring the pocket up into place on the caddy so that the right side of the pockets are up. Press and pin the pockets into place at the top unattached corners of both rows of pockets. Place the bottom pocket on the front piece, right side up, then pin into place. This pocket is stitched into place when the back of the caddy is attached to the front.

6. Pin the straps into place. The unseamed end of the straps should be set right up to the edge of the caddy front where indicated on the pattern. Stitch into place along the $^5/_8$" seam line, going over the seams twice to reinforce them.

7. Place the back piece on top of the front piece, right sides together, and pin into place. Stitch 3 sides of the caddy together as you would a pillowcase, leaving the top unseamed. Clip the corners, press the seams open, and turn it right side out. Press the fabric again. Sew all the pockets into place and leave the straps free to fasten around the car seat.

8. Fold down the seam allowances along the top of the caddy and press. Stitch near the edge with the sewing machine. Your caddy is now complete. Fasten the ends of the caddy around the front seats.

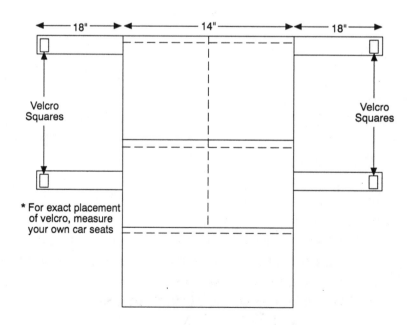